Thrall

Library of Congress Cataloging-in-Publications Data

Gevirtz, Susan.
    Thrall / Susan Gevirtz.
        p. cm.
    ISBN 978-0-942996-63-0
    I. Title.
    PS3557.E894T47 2007
    811'.54--dc22

                                    2007031170

The Post-Apollo Press
35 Marie Street
Sausalito, California 94965

Book design by Simone Fattal
Cover drawing by Etel Adnan

Typeset by Kathleen Wilkinson
in Goudy for the text
and Arno Pro and Garamond for the titling

Printed in the United States of America on acid-free paper.

Susan Gevirtz

Thrall

THE POST-APOLLO PRESS

Thrall

Acknowledgements

Versions of some of these poems first appeared in
*hemorragingimaging; untitled: A Journal of Prose Poetry;
POETRY SALZBURG REVIEW; Hambone.* Thanks
to the editors.

Thanks also to The Post-Apollo Press, Zaid Mesgna
W/Girgis, Clio Gevirtz, Norma Cole and Carrie Wicks.

This book, written from 2000 – 2002, is dedicated
to Clio.

All my life I have suffered from "geographical emotions."
Places are almost as real as people to me.

—Bryher

Contents

Thrall
  Chapter Book

Is person place or person

Dictionary Story

      for Norma Cole's "A Picture Book Without Pictures"

"Is the dictionary a story?"

Is word illustration of illumination?

              Untold thousands duplications

             Inchoate   [won't remember this Queen
Thralldom Dom

done to for maze

re-enchantment debased

retract that
picture
too much
escapes

Do not think of a land that will raise questions. Want assumes an object. About motion. Directions impossible. This is how you call Inexochta. Do something anathema to sleep. Something they do there. Also on the first day positing "first" as fist and "It was night. Small white lights hung on the arms of a staircase. Look, like a long bracelet," there where they can't leave the night alone. Always thinking there's another sky after this one

Lion in a Briefcase

He brought the lion home in a briefcase. Wasn't there
enough to tame already? The inconveniences recited.
As beautiful as the songs of indecipherable words sung
routinely so as to trick them into thinking never again
or not yet. What is small is not necessarily flat or
foldable or without great carnivorous capacity. Which
was probably the reason for bringing it home. In
Intelexa evening as comforting as the further danger
lodged in character. Or passing — the passing of style
or that which is mistaken as taken.

Is She Strong Enough to Turn on the Light?

Some questions refuse rest. You are not hostages you
are — touring the great cement lagoon drained of water
before it was made. Birds with magnets in their chests
alight on limbs, not moving for years.

"... from the mouth, and hands, the hair, above all the
gaze, an imperfect labiality surrounded him, she
witness...."

—Anne-Marie Albiach

She witness watching the place you are on TV The big
being at home.   enough   to turn

Hand by hand hand

by hand

into this Guess

whose

this

Character

In the land of Intelexa the beheaded face hovers above
following the body.

Water had dripped on to the page erasing the middles
of words. This construed as velocity. Here the
beheaded surpassed themselves, especially she who
had shaved clean the spinal nerve-endings. She who
had performed such a magnificent severance as to
persuade the sun of the first day to cast a static,
thousands of dust mote letters, a new element for the
sky's year pulled across the window. Read wonder of
wonder or "in the middle of your night, life." At the
right latitude a great condensation descends as in the
silent seam when one color bleeds into another. There
you can know proximity's hand

Etymology's Nemesis

Soaring and diving with the aquarium sharks casting
another shadow half imitation and half prebirth.
Drinking of this aquarium water tincture and thereby
knowing something happened. Thus reaching for the
dictionary. Inadequacy's tablet, one nervous twitch
before story's wish to subtract by including too many
particulars. Such soft wax of impression. A highly
sophisticated selection of pattern for which, in the
past, they had only the word "memory." In Intelexa
there is a saying, "Obfuscate so that the windshield's
film will clearly wash over you." This is not religious
maxim but the slay of time's desire to organize you
into a bonsai beyond recall.

The Anchored Lost

Then she appeared — the woman of one hundred
arms. First as still as tree branches, then windmilling,
but that is a word from the land next door. Then the
tale of the man who switched clothes with a Berber
woman and went looking for the lost city in the sand.
The desire to paint without making a picture. This
was the first story for the first day and one was aware
of that. "Sux - intravoxa," they muttered attempting
to get on with things. But all that was construed as
thing had reverted to sky at the slightest glance,
embarrassed sky.

In this Place which Legend Posits

A silence fell upon the land. More quiet than a map.
The sounds of place having to do with the
irreducibility and seamlessness of story. Airlines want
us to forget this. One body feeds sleep to the one next
to it. And the next imagines it as her own. For
example.

Paper Doll Day

The egg from the other chapter has followed us here.
"Revert" is the only word for it. A study of continuity
necessary. Of meals eaten as opposed to meals made,
read about, bought or imagined.
Flowering thyme takes too long to say.
Hand prints on cars.
Colander hours.
Archaeology you can't touch.
Ruffled hour, gravel hour

Bald Hatred

Don't speak to me of custom. Our concern is for habit, of which so little is known. But can we dwell outside the thumbprint? What outside may exist is not in Intelexa. Capitals, capitalization, a back street, a shuffled alphabet drying in the sun, not even. But a turning page may startle the air in a way previously undocumented. They adorn the walls of their homes with photographs of those turns. In this sense sealing the envelope becomes one of the most optimistic acts.

To Do

Yes it is the season of sales. But that does not mean
pull the chariot of the sun across vast window panes.
Even small children are immune there. Hand on
shoulder, descending steps, they look up and point at
the skywriting they love. To them it is the ghost of
breast milk waiting for the next. At night they throw
animal sponges in the air and wait till they drop on
someone's head

A Mother but Better

Reference suggests a solid ground. Still they continue
to do it. In the outside steppes of Inexochta an enormous
edifice built of edible aluminum is constructed at the
turn of the last season. Fat year or thin, full harvest or
meager, with or without the proper equipment, all
residents scale it, eating as they go. In the end another
town hovers, without its buildings, positing levitation
as a twin to dwelling. Later, they dive, landing by
somersault in deeply furrowed top soil. One was
overheard saying, "Photography slides right off of this"

The Assignments

Here is the time to tell about the assignments. It was
assumed that documentation was better done by
children on beaches. A kind of collecting and
sometimes reviewing. People did not have jobs but did
receive tasks. Instructed at all costs to annihilate
waiting. Anyone in love with impatience won't read
on. Suspense transcribes every act that has occurred
every morning of the year. A telescope the size of a
room. A day in the palm of a hand

Trading Names

They have a tradition of procession. Turning the light
off in the day sky. Holding candles and walking beside
the long river staying mute. Dropping their own
names into the water then picking up another. Each
winter a different name that lasts a year. The relief of
watching the clothes drift off. So we keep calling them
when they can't hear us.

Duplicity

One clothed form gave way to another unclothed.
One wave rolled out while one made of tin foil rolled
in. No shoreline, only the perfect match of breadcrumb
to bread.   But then I thought it was
Now I know it is   conditions conditions

Askance

There was no longer speaking when spoken to.
Reciprocation folded into a trunk and mailed to an
address of fifty years back. Buy a plot now before it's
too late. Not to bury in to aim at. "All gone," was the
anthem they couldn't get out of their heads

Chosen

Some were chosen as widows at the age of five. Only they you will find if you come here. Then a zig zag movement, so missed us. Flying on your back roadside decanted. Air decorated by heads on stakes. The sea, the great eraser. Arms of the first, Cessna infested sea. All historical account has gone begging — begging as return. All accent disappears as the girls learn more words.

Avatar Ship

Avatar ship blowing home without wind. But don't
follow from line to line. She sang on the radio or we
had   we rode   we ride   over there   pretend words
all over the dinner. This is how, by way of the roof of
the mouth, some survive a foot in two oceans. In
Intelexa it is understood that cause is an opposite
inform. That is what is meant by unable to get away.
Or imagine a round table, the fantasist directing a
cat's cradle later called ours in a future already strewn
with the cast-off and under construction.

Light of Day

Doubtless air will uphold. This the flat landscape of
no escape. Fish under rug, tongue nailed to the wall.
They have no prisons, only public monuments.

Living in the I don't know all deaf ears are upon us.
Light of day by watch us whoever we are. Air turns to
turnstile. Each miss is named adoration a wreath on
the neck of a side door. Avoid the need to ask. They
call this criminal here.

To Not Name

Forgetting something means then sirens enter the
sound-proof room. The hold off on remembering or
naming olympics. Those who win are awarded a
surgery trophy. The only incision performed is
shoulder replacement. Taking out the scapula and
putting in the wingspan of a bald eagle. This way
extinction is avoided. Flight is still not possible but
again and again the recipient experiences lift-off.

Prophecy's Accident

A little square of fire flipped with a spatula. A little
place expanding under running water. Nowhere but
only
destination's imaginable
breakfast   "In dreams, a writing tablet signifies a
woman, since it receives the imprint of all kinds of
letters..." —Artemidorus

                              nothing hate hates

                         more than nothing

indifference enslaved

                              little square
of reception

Captivations

Way off in the diamond fields nothing but prelude.
Miles of shiny black plastic covered with holes through
which a little green breathes if you can call it breath.
This is their apocalypse, no aged women or planets
littered with rocket wreckage. Dim moisture, weather
of collapsed lung, surface noise as bedtime story, and
you in the next chapter or the next.

0 – 12   The Walk-in Books
postscript to Thrall

Provisional

It's called the sleeping dragon — tubes and chains to prevent entering

                    a situation

Commerce of breakfast

and the satisfy of execution is

glee   house

noose

adornment

it is

all

about about

plastic bag jewelry

predilection, prediction

or prophecy?

12

each month the chapter of a year
into which deep furrows had been plowed
and seedlings dropped from the air
alphabetic   to harvest or not
                              after twelve turns

twelve bars, doors between

The Endurances

A bookshelf

    with a drawer in it

        in the drawer a
    small statue on its back

the parents waiting for
it to turn over

rocks swimming upstream

so wash the fishing angle

Twelve books visit the sea edge

decrepitudes recited

twelve books out-loud so we can put our hands in

while listening to your hearts keep time
with the sea

under hood of sky
pulled tight all around
grotto accompaniment
A terrace so close to sea
our feet were often wet

What did we eat there? Who swept
and boiled water?
What word

makes a three dimensional book?

the cancel word

now spelled on its back

Time of Orders

Proffered   pilfered

ignited   stamped out remains

in the Suffice

sky biting   tidings

sequestered
under

razor moon

Foretell

"So frail is judgment
It must light up, an overseer
With, some truckling in hell
A song that lovers' heads
Ear to, and an ear foretell"
—Zukofsky, Non Ti Fidar
[Never Trust that evil man, from Mozart's Don Giovanni]

"In opera poetry must be the obedient daughter of music"
—Mozart

When I was

in the sky who

looked away at

exuberance of randomness

"When I was in my mother" whose constellation face

dying from response

repose dies of dream life

sleep bright as day

when we have all died out and

there are no more last words

a dead star a bright static

when we were just born

among us I asked

for visitation

or was it volume

so I could tell you what

you can't tell

to the one who looked

alike happened happened

demolition drone light fingers sleep's

husbandry awake to coma

traffic dirge the secret history of

the provisional everything

exiled asks about

navigation underwritten happened

required expired undertaken

asks about forms

paper plane paper fire afloat

everything asks and

to come back

one trail melted in snow, one repeated by ants,

one a trajectory of

It is said

underwriter underwater

the required bread of

prophecy's dominion

It is said it will be

like this

vacant decanter filled

with profession

take everything

trappings in the trappings cave

tied with

immediacy

where you carry the satchel

over one shoulder

once in

a life

time's washed up

target practice reduce

cause to cause until all that's left

is distant

skyline of inaction

So talk to me now

in any sentence

structure you can

one ear on the rise

some constellation seen only

at this season

season of not often

of only

Forgiving Light
The Semblances the Resemblances

"I have lowered the plot to reveal the ground"
—Clark Coolidge

Newcomer composing in
hair

a little collapse
a little beefed-up moment then

what they call
forgiving light

A little comment. A little comet.
Already fear in the body. Probably she put it there.
There is only a way in, not a way out and another and
another and another all
the way
past the voices
above the bed
and through another
ceiling
another sky
after another

disembodied in your hands. Send air back

you are your many appearances

hypnogogue   demagogue

You appeared as land but were an act

as face but were land disgorged

50

coward the ground

recursive cursive

that future

written could vanish

wish or be banished

swerve or wave of a hand

miss and dismissal

rest your head
on a pillow of dirt

Shay and Slay

Shay and slay are

two twins

What did she

say?

That's a riddle

Riddle till you

drop

At a remove

skirting

The crater

without contempt

All is quiet. All done. All said
that could be said

that could the done
be said

Terrible Parable

Down at the bottom of the sky

your memory planet whipping

out of orbit.   The brotherhood

of procedure cannot construe

the not-next rodeo

Streets were paved with doubt

inside one chest

another and inside

that a trunk. Inside

the trunk a nest of alligator eggs

serving a stronger and smaller

sun no more

of your organs on my platter

Unworthy is hamburger

to compete with steak

Take direction

walking into the first

of twelve books

Fire Station No. 7

There is no hurry up
There is no hurry late
Only the draw of time's
mule chariot

Medusa strip-searched
in a small alcove
littered with switchblades
and Mnemosyne's libretto

Way in the night in
the middle of nights
you do this
When you
wave circle dash line
back of your every
she too
is forgot
forgetting song

say she is

mimic but one ratchet

up turn

your back

she witness and he

falling over

neon impression

enough of enough?
what the quotation quotes?

Reverse Marketing

Why the balloon

so big and the

head so small?

Why is the pin so

invisible and

the air so palpable

Why is proportion

craving vision

question of

peeling off one

face to reveal another

and again and again as

the sun never rests

so skin has its

night and day

The official story sits

next to the initial story

where on the inside

of her thigh

he wanted

to initialize her

She put things in bags and went back to the market.
Canned goods, milk, grapes, bread, all returned to
their bins, shelves, cases

Under the Impression

More abject than abnegation. More listless than
anodyne. Anodyne, she of the hundred headdresses,
she whose name surpasses naming, damning them
with the 100 suns revolving around one planet. Or
going down on the street, like on a person on his knees
praying. A city in which all blue cars levitate, the next
day all red. Driving through the air singing "all I
wanted was not adoration." It was not coloration
either. Slave to response, steering wheel ripped out at
the root like so many vegetables in an irrational early
harvest of root canal

Moratorium

but not bitterly

not with coercion

someone's

little topknot

tied

to a beginning is not

where it started

name scrawled on scraps

you great precursor

peruser, trappist

empathy's carnage
cornucopia dumpster

Speechless Dalliance

That is my arm

I forgot at the door

instrument of nothing

to say

Vetiver   Mollusk   Gorgonzola
Honey   Semen
's speechless postscript

fragment to part II
found years later

among the future
I remember

Out the other

side of night

out out and out until

turns to turnstile

turnstile to stretcher and stretcher

into the talking insect

A Plot of Land

for Gad Hollander

Embark

bright splash

young girl's bare feet

walking on figs

Dream be with me

save me the way S G R &

L survived

Here before

you

go put one cherry

back

on the tree

In film we believe the weather

It was a staunch land

not a wrinkle lay upon it

It was new sheets

making a match for skin

"It was a quiet conversion in

twenty minutes actual time

an afternoon in film time"

rubbing years together
like dollar bills

It was the Gatekeeper counting
years like cash

Dedicated Darkness

"What I hope to be a dedicated darkness"
                          —Clark Coolidge

If I were a

I'd

overheard

departure and rehearse

calling it developmental regardless of age and calling it

good-bye regardless of return

Forced Speech

"Your stinginess with you"
Thus blunted muzzle
face hand-held or

Stain the words
overrated over rated
or overate together
as umbilical as dinner
your etiquette you're again in
your own gullet

        Yes, ice cream is
        made of snow

        Yes, tree branches
        make
        wind yes and yes
        and yes

        makes

        bedlam
        bedlam

        my love
        water makes
        glass so the
        windshield is

a glacier you can
see yourself in

Stain the words
inconsolable

the letters

oppose within
one a fight

breaks out venom's

motion

reading's solace
place

Tyrana Detritus

YOU are an aviary

YOU are tundra

and You go on vacation
to a resort where guests learn to

talk like dolphins

Throw triangle dice

in the eternity between the birth

of twins

Tale of the Insatiate

"...as though paralyzed in an enchantment..."
—Anne-Marie Albiach

the injured the never
to recover
the sewn up
sky stitched with new stars

outcast   outland   outlaw's

time's double blind twice

antennae territories   zero o'clock

complicity's dignity remastered

Do mistakes exist? Forgettable as cash

filled with antidote

to sleep revenge's revenge

take back point blank

by the pond pond

children mistaken

betters sleep up by the house

cloaked in fever

in marvel

Deciphretude

*On the flyleaf he found the name of the owner Ursula
Reuber and then noticed pencil marks in the table of
contents; every few lines one letter had a dot. When he
put together the letters he had a sentence "I am here too."*

—New York Times Magazine,
"The Good Germans,"
February 13, 2000

Every moment the language of action is akin to research.

—David Ward

The Name of Our Walk

"...the stars overwhelm the stars"
—Heidegger

nearness is close to us

The madonna who

wants something from nothing
sits on her miracle

A gaggle of girls

put embryos in socks

> We so be again   gen
> and around the garden do

> and oscillate too
> when another
>   wans
> How if winged too
>   do?

Gate   Gate   Paragate

Here too

        Flyleaf

              half life   shelf life

          shell life

            Embark

          bright splash

        In film we believe the weather

a young girl's feet walking on figs

            Dream be with me

          save me the way S G R &

              L survived

               before walking out the door
"Here, you put one cherry back on the tree"

and so you will remain

Under drop sky

        into low-ceilinged sleep
houndstooth, blue and black checked

A guard slipped him a volume of Rilke's poetry

                     between eyelid and eye

        draw a line
        in sand

                        ///

Egg donor>

<Ghostwriter

surgery

forgery

OF

Epiphany

unreportable apostrophe   unreadable   inaudible

outside the polis

outline timeline

metronomic oceanic

Sundial's default object

^>

        yet by crumb's scrap infinite
conversation provides its measure exacts its pound
from <><><>

        Bring me my scapegoat and I will feed it
Eat

        Promise not   escape
ordained   entertained on I.V. milk

        Succor
Foresight

        born celibate   rebate

        = age

a terrible relapse into

scenic drive

       memory's future as error's

hour overwritten

                               horror un
name the timed
There is not enough quantity to represent

gravity's resignation
< >
<
<
>

                        ///

Our Inclination Chambers

Sometimes a white ship

                                      sometimes a split
second   you a

                                              time
passing is   I will

                                    paddling
over the black water
                              No one could see us but
                  right angles   anticipation's sick rise
off swells of water

                  pummel the

                  trees pummel

                  your jaw

land cracks and animals
can't cross

This description   wind in the chest cache
arson
criss-crossing true deception
     genuflecting to "How that state of mind was
photographed...." —D. Richardson

              She pulled a gun at the water

Oh. She gave me triangles
to prop up the space between neck and shoulders
What else did she give you?
A bowl full arranged; the dissolve deranged; the
cardboard of "The geraniums still make the whole cliff,
cardboard." —H.D.   countless, nameless lists, she gave
me fraudulent miles

Terms of Identification

either which

or because

To compose   sing   recite   copy
set

as sun or table

to become infirm

why he does not continue

expedition   disinclination's reason

imprecise precision

Says Blancandrin "I swear by my right"

Clarin, Estramariz and Eudropin

topiary

Turoldus

C O P Y I S T   by the wayside

                          detritus all

                     explanation
                  inaction or commit

                     sleight of hand

Out of Order

my velvet, a booklet, next year as I was

saying subpoenaed by doubt but

what is the depth of that how does

it inform

watching the painting with binoculars

motion detector

taking the pulse of dirt

underground workers

cherries balanced on their heads

[mistaken for procession   list —   —

No: Fifty-two species of birds talking
103 different tongues

while   It was a great hurricane
   and we were   bound to be hit by
jet wash in the anguish

unmoors proposition

faster   [starve

—pulling up
at the tank

How it looks What it's made of each
color has seven songs each song has all colors in it
Each color orders no answer

Doubt and doubtless our chariot
wheels run over countless absolute quiets

nameless not
mistaken

Now all sevens the seven of seventy-three

transfusion's shadow

It was a great hurricane named weather detector
binocular painter

///

Rumor X's 3

picture sound

before seen before

   eight cauldrons which were beakers which were
shark tanks   which required defense a cry issued
from the wings name of a dream a family a history in
which all the nights were recalled for inspection
draping day in doubt out of breath out of reach

This
   the
dark before
the dark
This the
rouge
the mice
collect then scatter
prepare them

This the diction
   hearken
lark pie   This
      phantom
close to the lie
This rhyme before time
   so off to bed
This bed of seizure
   by this they are
   fed

Ritual in Transfigured Time

after Maya Deren

Back-story
stroking re-enactment

hypochondria's reverie
closer and closer precision of description equals
closer to cure

Or to dispel? The Story of Far
birds like skylark and Buick Skylark

what is being said translated into what is being said

Three days omitted from the week
and in those days adultery, robbery, memory without
accountability

///

We ran out of

order so we ran

away together

into a radio

into a land

where we ate water

with chopsticks ate

air

We
know the
inventory

of purgatory

Now what
is
eating your heart
out of my palm

This

way of speaking

this sudden

tear

fabric of

We know forecast
the forecast key
ice we know ice
weather closed around us
a circuit of copper clouds
trapped us

in the summer house
in the summer
sometimes seasons are stuck
rope around time's
neck

but enough

telling cease

cease to resist

paean to
some kind of impediment

surgical ana gory
grammar's grandeur
rubble of intentions

gag rule
many the sea
scrabble squander

///

Unannounced

Helicopter   Canticle   Soundtrack
rhapsodic episodic

                                                    Dog
Star   dying by day
                        by night outdistanced
                    by the visible

                                        father licks
granddaughter's cheek

laughs it off

                                    Displacement to
attachment by ailment
                            an eating without taste
that is storytelling

AVAIL   No avail   flat line
accompaniment book of

The New Paralysis next to Our Reliquarium under M on
the shelf

will relinquish meals'
secret

Times No remains
stammer multiply
slice ahead splice

                                                          riptide

molecules
                                              accident's

windshield
                                          page talking at

blacking out
                                            talking back

Bandwidth

Example can be an heirloom of junk: two jewelry
boxes with the grandmother and grandfather's hands
still inside

Because shock of the new temporarily eliminates
distraction   There is ever hunger   little known
There are temperatures of sleep

                                        said owl or Apollo
trapped in the house

                    stand on a papier-mache hill

                            skate the drained reservoir
speed at which

        replaces

    velocity's lyric

                        overheard

                    Ingratitude rears its beautiful mane

                        skid on which   habit of speech

                    delete certainty parts
set course

"There is no wordlessness"
—Jakobson

unnumbered counting

late correspondence

White out

limbic   nimbus   voice's
calculus

shorthand on the
tarmac

shortwave why
does air stay in the sky

Draw a circle in sand
jam a square inside it
Did I hear
correctly said
use a stick   erase
demise
demise of
sea bottom
demise of explanation

You get to hate something
and tolerate it
fricative   modified   broken
I give you these for use
   The Things They Carried
hailstorm of titles
tools wishing

"To be punished before committing a fault." —Zizek
  to be published

92

///

before cognition definition region of thought's

/formation

/precedes

prophecy's diagnosis   hanging gold coins in the air
and waiting for them to hatch   mouthpiece for
backbeat   anything is understatement

I made a little persistence some called a line numbers
and heat ludic
numbers and heat ludic
little display of infection in front of the child and so
we know that you are your own clue/ Sleep /yes, the
first
separation ever last

anagory / yes I have been reading
forbidden

the first is surgical stagnations

scrabble squander

grammar's grandeur rubble's intentions
gag rule   marry the sea
turns to porridge or stolen eggs

And then the partings that are not a story

                parting of water

                parting of night

                life in parts

                the partings began

                partings of

the space between the stars   not empty
expanse
informative

                              prior to

form   intolerate union
departure start again

                          Impediment Story

                           as if without

                          history

                                    [not
                          approach [calamity

///

94

Forced Speech

pig   blockhead

never can   cast off

                    "fictive character the remoter potency"

gone there   everywhere

                                        Anxiety's undoing
silent witness

before lost

              was

Under arrest

                                        Paginate Name:

"We never shall. We shall drive
     As the years drive
Into the snow bitten stunt of woods
     where mother waits"   —Bromige

                                                  that plank
my velvet booklet
next year   saves us measurement

                 we were watching the painting with
binoculars   parade and the wave breaking on our
heads

Human Shield

         One
              untampered

         One
              overlaps
              (repeating)
              chorus

         One
              enjambed
              condensed
              (without space)

         One
              expanded

Moat Hotel refrain

Space and singularity   not dragged voice   no
chorus   diurnal

without naming and ramifications thereof

timbre   tone   cavernous   attack/diminish
echo spare

                          Open all Moat Hotel
rooms at once

dug up comportment   burned repeat

Bidding

Sentinel awake
so sleepers keep sleep

Said she she said the said

Right of return fiasco

Stone sirens

Partial   Wonder always a first encounter

creates the object that is already and decimates the
there that was

                                             first sight

never dislodged
sleeps through love   One last

ride on the night ferry   in glass slippers called
never touch

the ground

as the recent present

contacts us

by intercom

Debt Service

                                    Attribution
Karelia

                    ice floe

              transaction

broadcast

Remastered

Bathed in floodlights

To kneel beside his car

Call it expanse

        call it   occupation   name of name

stone sirens
stone's slow silence

misfire   castaway
                           puzzlements
                           whereby

Side body

Fret

drastic dramatic

      So sideswiped or slapped head on

So no infancy   history by

    rumor collision

      Reception's auction

///

Meanwhile

          queued up

          railroading you

          hearsay

have always

thought becomes event

annihilating content

"Becoming an entity, an infinitive"
—Deleuze & Parnet

devoid of cause implication's lifespan
        speed of rock

        speed of helicopter blades the translation of
helicopter blades slicing the sky

makes paranomasia   without definition I can find so

Hoarding the hopes of long lost loves is how
he made a killing crossing the river Styx called Stockmarket

Everything its use everyone in time

Selling your area code so someone will call
buying proposition is one position

Candles to the stars on the road to Look Back

SOME SOURCES

"Thrall Chapter Book" and "0 – 12 The Walk-in Books"

  Norma Cole, "A Picture Book Without Pictures,"
    first published in *Conjunctions*, No. 35, 2000;
    forthcoming in *To Be At Music*, Factory
    School, 2007.

  Anne-Marie Albiach, *A Discursive Space,
    Interviews with Jean Daive*, translated by
    Norma Cole, Burning Deck, 1999.

  Artemidorus, *Oneirocritica*, translation and
    commentary by Robert J. White, Banton
    Press, 1992.

                    "Deciphretude"

  The Song of Roland, translated by Patricia Terry,
    MacMillan, 1965.

  Martin Heidegger, *Discourse on Thinking*,
    translated by John M. Anderson and
    E. Hans Freung, Harper, 1966.